MW00933699

WE HOPE YOU ENJOY THIS COLORING BOOK!

THIS BOOK BELONGS TO:

I'M IN
HUMAN
RESOURCES
WHAT'S YOUR
SUPER
POWER?

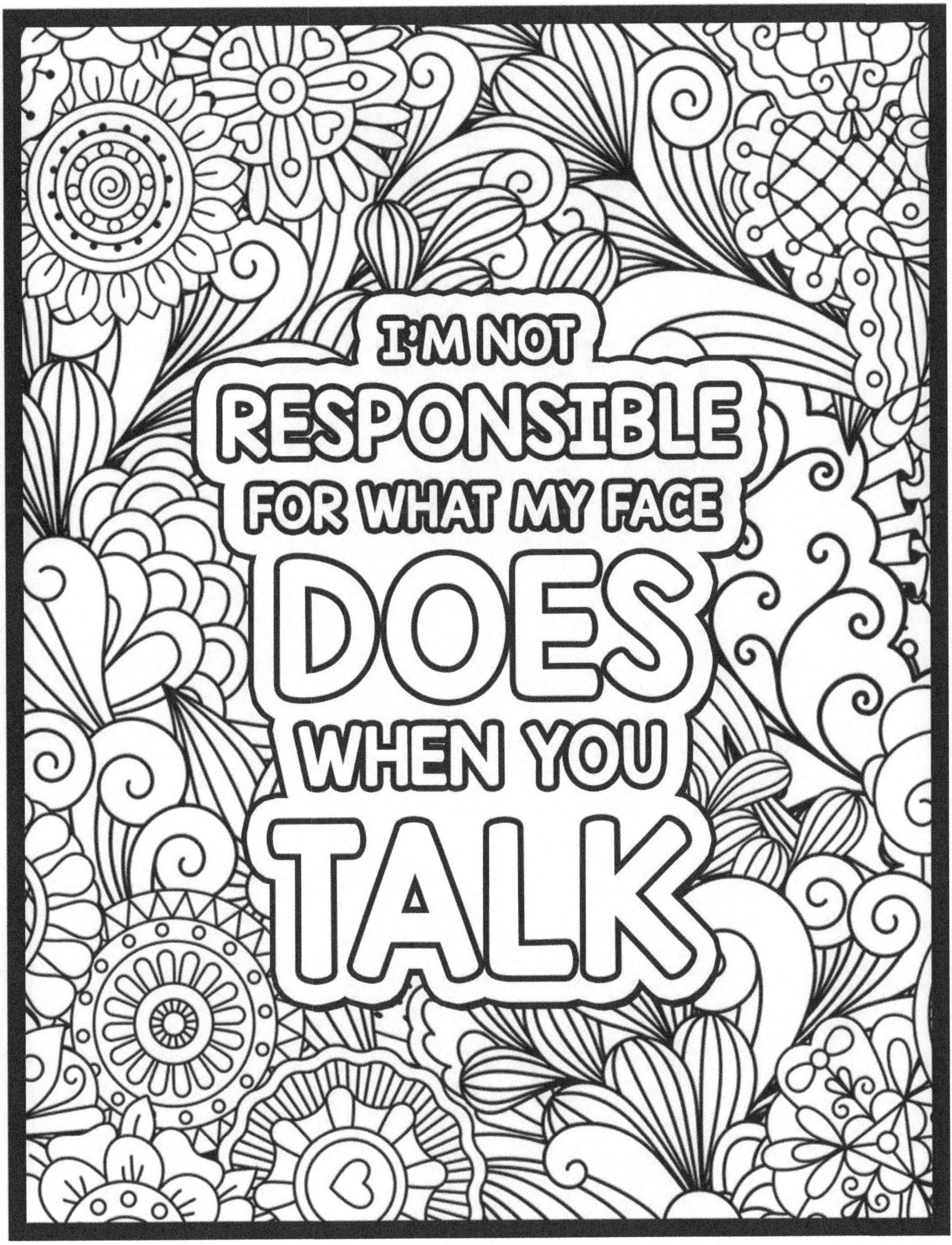
I'M NOT
RESPONSIBLE
FOR WHAT MY FACE
DOES
WHEN YOU
TALK

I NEVER DREAMED
I'D BE
A SUPER
COOL
HUMAN
RESOURCE
BUT HERE I'M
KILLIN' IT

I MISS
YOUR
STUPID
FACE
TODAY

I'm Sorry
the Nice
HR
is on
Vacation!

THIS DAY WAS
SUCH AS A
CLUSTERF*CK
AND I DON'T
GIVE A SH!T

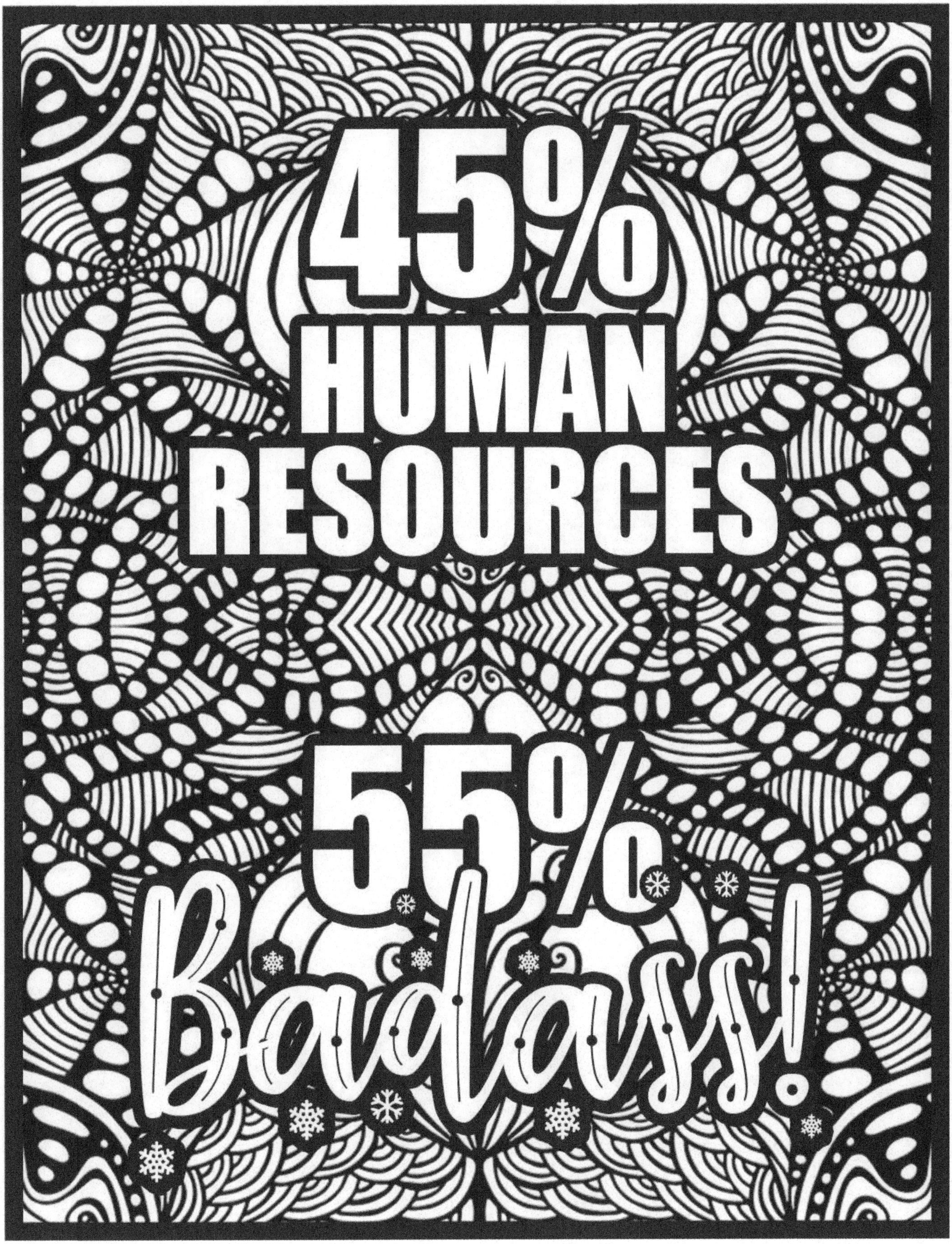
45%
HUMAN
RESOURCES
55%
Badass!

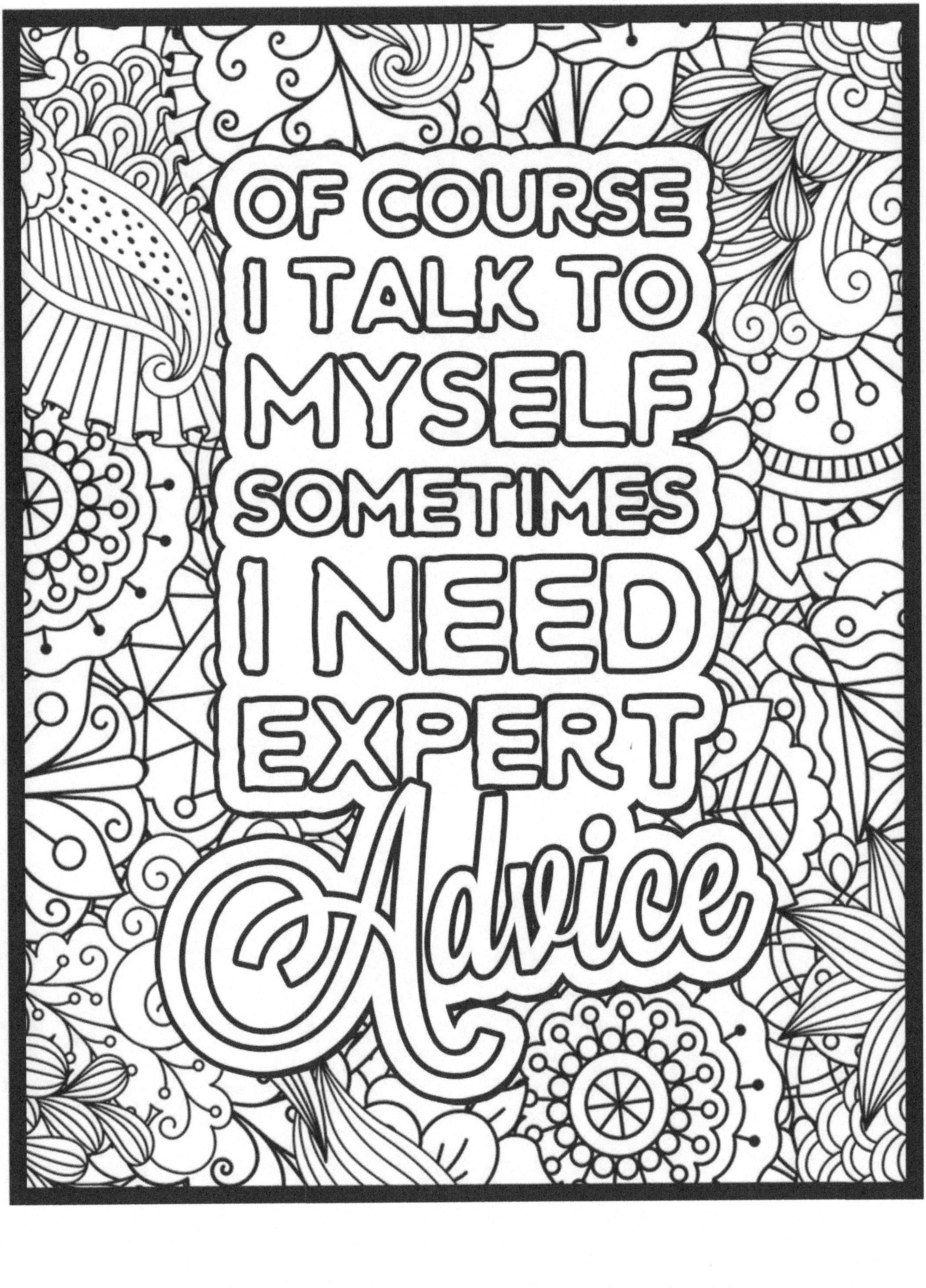
OF COURSE
I TALK TO
MYSELF
SOMETIMES
I NEED
EXPERT
Advice

DON'T MAKE
ME USE MY
HR
Voice

STFU!
TO SAVE TIME
JUST ASSUME
I'M ALWAYS
RIGHT

LOOK AT ME
BECOMING IN
HUMAN
RESOURCES
AND
SHIT

Essential
AF!

WORLD'S
Okayest
HR

I've 101
Problems
But
Coloring
Ain't One

THIS
HUMAN
RESOURCE
NEEDS A
NAP!

I'm a
Nice Person
Just Don't
Push My
Bit*h
Button!

YOU MUST BE
MISTAKING ME
FOR A
HR
WHO GIVES A
SH!T

I NEED A
MOTHER
F*CKIN'
DRINK

IT'S A
HUMAN
RESOURCES
THING
YOU'D NOT
UNDERSTAND

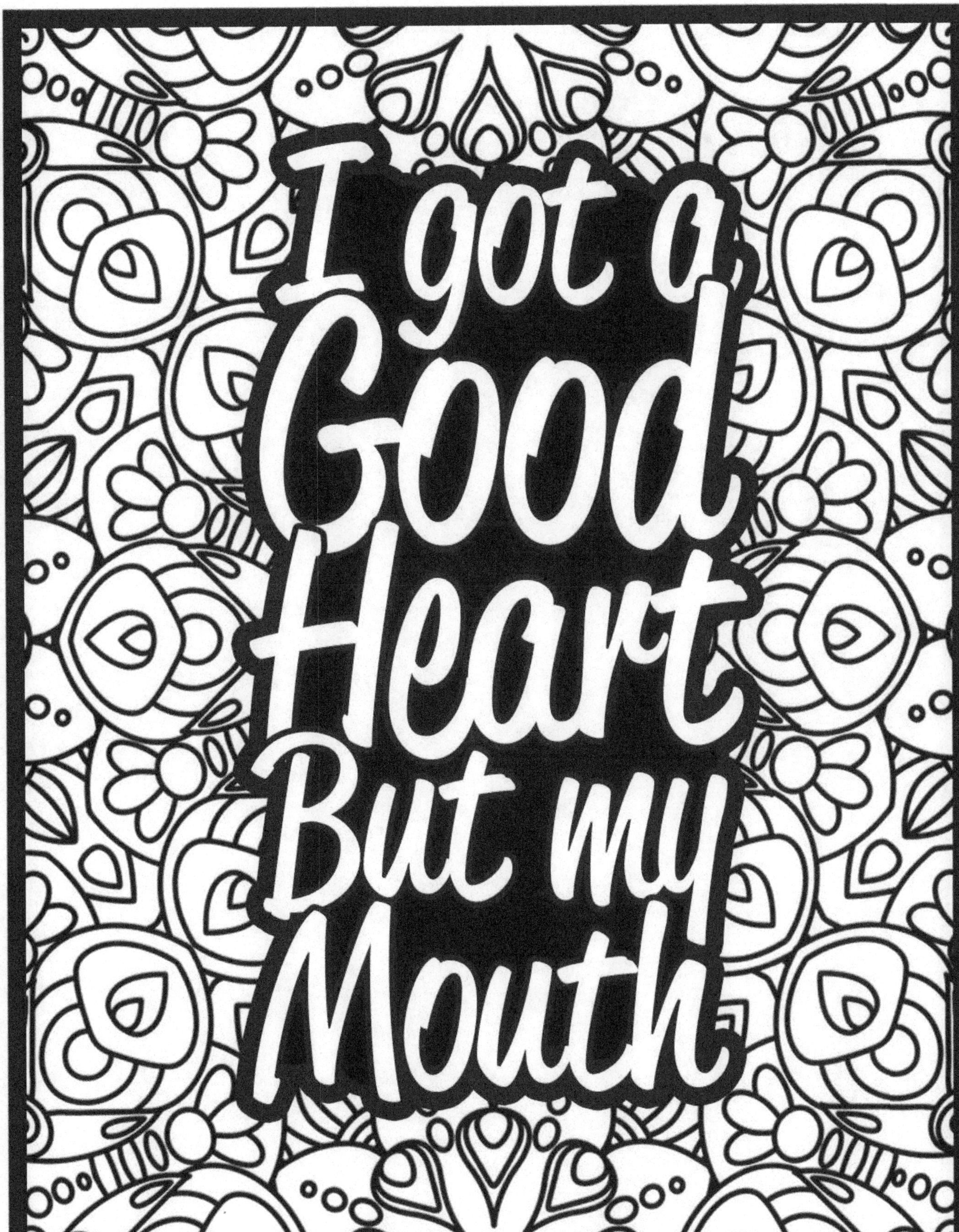
I got a Good Heart But my Mouth

Made in the USA
Las Vegas, NV
01 December 2023

81931480R00024